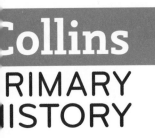

Collins
PRIMARY
HISTORY

Sign
Individuals
Pupil Book

C000179050

Working together to:
IVY HOUSE SCHOOL
inspire, nurture, empower

IVY HOUSE SCHOOL
MOORWAY LANE
LITTLEOVER
DERBY
DE23 2FS
TEL: 01332 777920

Sue Temple | Alf Wilkinson

William Collins' dream of knowledge for all began with the publication of his first book in 1819.
A self-educated mill worker, he not only enriched millions of lives, but also founded a flourishing publishing house. Today, staying true to this spirit, Collins books are packed with inspiration, innovation and practical expertise. They place you at the centre of a world of possibility and give you exactly what you need to explore it.

Collins. Freedom to teach.

Published by Collins
An imprint of HarperCollins*Publishers*
The News Building
1 London Bridge Street
London
SE1 9GF

Browse the complete Collins catalogue at
www.collins.co.uk

© HarperCollins*Publishers* Limited 2019

Maps © Collins Bartholomew 2019

10 9 8 7 6 5 4 3 2 1

ISBN 978-0-00-831080-6

All rights reserved. No part of this publication may be reproduced, stored in a retrieval system, or transmitted in any form by any means, electronic, mechanical, photocopying, recording or otherwise, without the prior written permission of the Publisher or a licence permitting restricted copying in the United Kingdom issued by the Copyright Licensing Agency Ltd, Barnard's Inn, 86 Fetter Lane, London, EC4A 1EN.

British Library Cataloguing-in-Publication Data
A catalogue record for this publication is available from the British Library.

Authors: Sue Temple and Alf Wilkinson
Publisher: Lizzie Catford
Product developer: Natasha Paul
Copyeditor: Sally Clifford
Indexer: Jouve India Private Ltd
Proofreader: Nikky Twyman
Image researcher: Alison Prior
Map designer: Gordon MacGilp
Cover designer and illustrator: Steve Evans
Internal designer: EMC Design
Typesetter: Jouve India Private Ltd
Production controller: Rachel Weaver
Printed and bound by Martins the Printers

MIX
Paper from
responsible sources
FSC
www.fsc.org
FSC™ C007454

This book is produced from independently certified FSC™ paper to ensure responsible forest management.

For more information visit:
www.harpercollins.co.uk/green

The publishers gratefully acknowledge the permission granted to reproduce the copyright material in this book. Every effort has been made to trace copyright holders and to obtain their permission for the use of copyright material. The publishers will gladly receive any information enabling them to rectify any error or omission at the first opportunity.

Contents

Introduction

All through history people have been doing amazing things to help each other. Some people have been famous, like kings, queens and leaders of their countries. Others have been much less known known but, in some ways, have done things which are even more important and significant than famous people. By reading about the people in this book, you will learn about just a few of these people, who were from all around the world.

When we talk about these people, we use the word 'significant'. This means they have done something that is interesting and important. However, everyone has different ideas about who should be called 'significant'. You may know people in your own town or local area who you feel are important and interesting. You could look at the following reasons to help you decide if the person you are thinking about should be called 'significant'.

Reasons for a person being significant

If he/she:

- changed events at the time they lived.
- improved lots of people's lives – or made them worse.
- changed people's ideas.
- had a long-lasting impact on its country or the world.
- had been a very good example, or a very bad example, to other people of how to live or behave.

Adapted from Dawson 2017

We hope this book will help you to learn about a few different people you may not have heard about before. We think they are significant – but you might not agree. Have fun!

Timeline of events

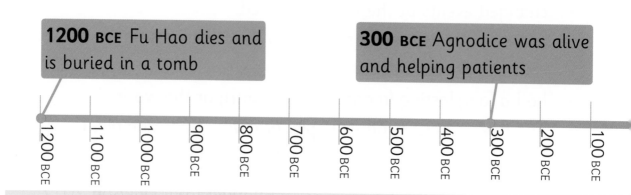

1200 BCE Fu Hao dies and is buried in a tomb

300 BCE Agnodice was alive and helping patients

1200 BCE | 1100 BCE | 1000 BCE | 900 BCE | 800 BCE | 700 BCE | 600 BCE | 500 BCE | 400 BCE | 300 BCE | 200 BCE | 100 BCE

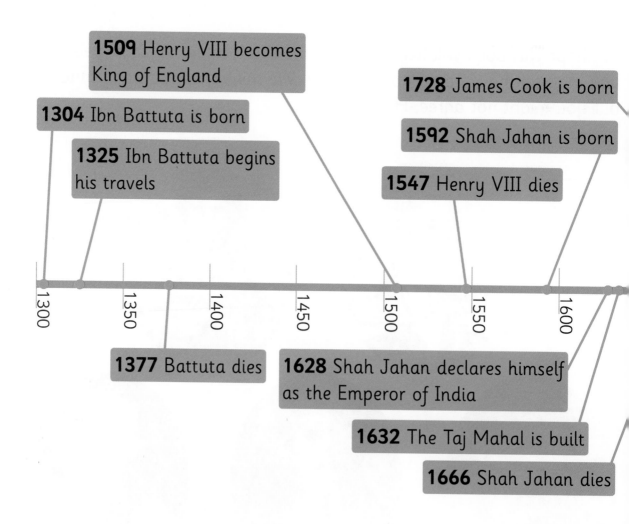

1509 Henry VIII becomes King of England

1304 Ibn Battuta is born

1325 Ibn Battuta begins his travels

1728 James Cook is born

1592 Shah Jahan is born

1547 Henry VIII dies

1300 | 1350 | 1400 | 1450 | 1500 | 1550 | 1600

1377 Battuta dies

1628 Shah Jahan declares himself as the Emperor of India

1632 The Taj Mahal is built

1666 Shah Jahan dies

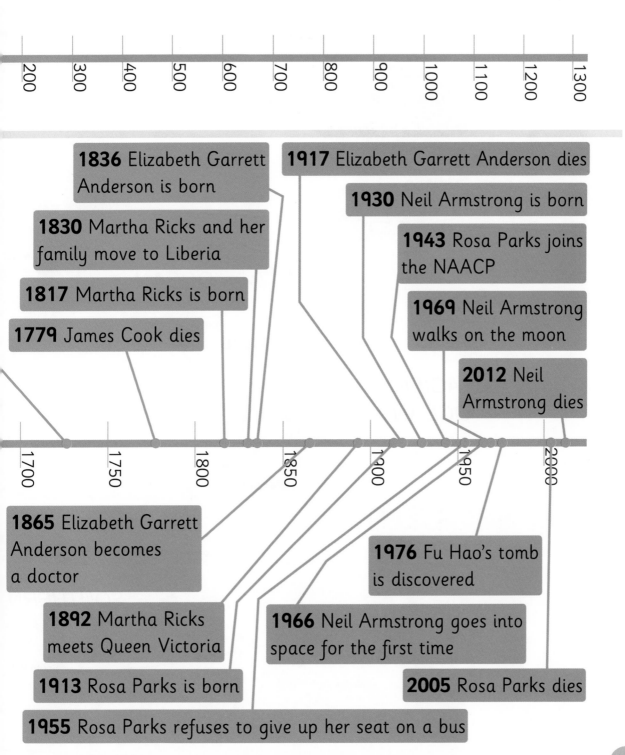

200   300   400   500   600   700   800   900   1000   1100   1200   1300

1836 Elizabeth Garrett Anderson is born

1917 Elizabeth Garrett Anderson dies

1830 Martha Ricks and her family move to Liberia

1930 Neil Armstrong is born

1817 Martha Ricks is born

1943 Rosa Parks joins the NAACP

1779 James Cook dies

1969 Neil Armstrong walks on the moon

2012 Neil Armstrong dies

1700   1750   1800   1850   1900   1950   2000

1865 Elizabeth Garrett Anderson becomes a doctor

1976 Fu Hao's tomb is discovered

1892 Martha Ricks meets Queen Victoria

1966 Neil Armstrong goes into space for the first time

1913 Rosa Parks is born

2005 Rosa Parks dies

1955 Rosa Parks refuses to give up her seat on a bus

World map

ARCTIC OCEAN

RUSSIA

KAZAKHSTAN

MONGOLIA

JAPAN

PACIFIC
OCEAN

CHINA

RKEY

TURKMENISTAN

SYRIA

AFGHANISTAN

IRAQ

IRAN

RDAN

PAKISTAN

NEPAL

SAUDI
ARABIA

OMAN

INDIA

MYANMAR

AN

ERITREA YEMEN

THAILAND

VIETNAM

PHILIPPINES

ETHIOPIA

SRI
LANKA

SOMALIA

MALAYSIA

KENYA

Equator

TANZANIA

INDIAN
OCEAN

INDONESIA

PAPUA NEW
GUINEA

SOLOMON
ISLANDS

OZAMBIQUE

VANUATU

MADAGASCAR

AUSTRALIA

NEW
ZEALAND

9

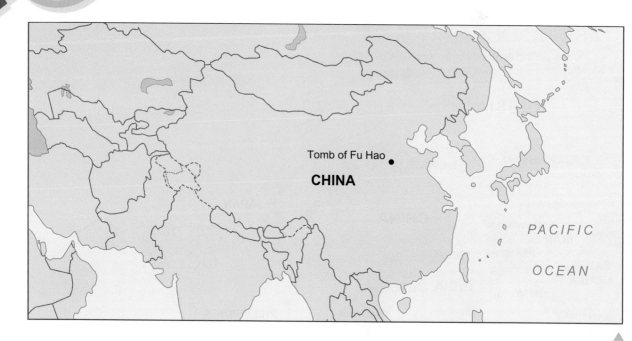

Map showing the location of Fu Hao's tomb

Who was Fu Hao?

In 1976, workmen in China came across a tomb. It seemed to be very old. It was full of precious things. It turned out to date from the Shang dynasty, and was over 3000 years old.

Conquered:

This is when one tribe beat another in a war or battle.

We know from the ox bones that the woman buried in the tomb was called Fu Hao. She was one of the wives of Emperor Wu Ding. He had over 60 wives! When a Shang ruler **conquered** another tribe, he married one of their princesses to keep the peace. Wu Ding conquered lots of tribes and so had many wives. No one knows what Fu Hao looked like, as there are no pictures of her. All the pictures we have are guesses drawn by modern-day artists.

This is Fu Hao's tomb today

Wu Ding was very fond of Fu Hao. We know this from the things he said about her on the ox bones. We also know she was very important and rich, because of all the things buried with her in her tomb.

We think Fu Hao might have looked like this

What was happening then?

The **Shang** ruled part of China, around the Yellow River, a very long time ago, from around 1700 BCE to around 1050 BCE. Some of them lived in big cities, but many lived and farmed in the countryside. The Yellow River often flooded, so they built **dykes and dams** to try to control the floods. The Shang are famous for being the first rulers of China we know a lot about, and also for their skills at making items from **bronze**, and for their beautiful **carvings**. They also had a strong army.

Shang:
The people who were in charge in China for just over 500 years.

Dykes and dams:
These were like walls built to keep the water from a river or lake in one place, or to move the water to where they wanted it to go.

Bronze:
This is a material made mainly from copper, with some tin and often other metals added to make it stronger.

Carvings:
This is when you use a sharp edge to make marks on an object, sometimes writing or pictures.

▲
Examples of the artefacts found in Fu Hao's tomb. From the left: jade bird, jade elephant, bronze bird

Before taking any important decision, the Shang would consult their gods. Only special people could do this. They used bones from **oxen**. They would carve their question on  the bones. Then they would heat up a piece of metal, and place this on the bone, which would crack. The shape of the cracks would answer their question for them. We know lots about the Shang from bones that archaeologists have discovered.

Oxen:

These are large male cattle which are trained to pull carts and ploughs.

There were over 2000 items inside Fu Hao's tomb, many made of bronze and **jade**. These included over 100 weapons, mostly axes and knives. Sixteen servants were buried around the tomb, as well as six dogs. Were the dogs hunting dogs, or pets? We are not really sure. There were also lots of ox bones with writing on, which 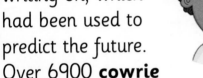 had been used to predict the future. Over 6900 **cowrie shells**, which the Shang used as money, were also found. In the middle of the tomb, there were the remains of a woman who had been buried around 1200 BCE.

Jade:

This is a precious stone which is green. It is very hard, and the Chinese liked to carve special objects from it.

Cowrie shells:

The shells of sea snails, which are very smooth and shiny, and used like money in the Shang dynasty.

What happened next?

What else do we know about Fu Hao? We know her name, which is very unusual for a woman in Shang China. We know she was very important, and probably a very  strong person — she was one of 60 wives, yet she was the one Wu Ding trusted the most. She was a **priest**, who used the ox bones to decide what to do. Again, this was very unusual for a woman.

Priest:

This is a religious leader, someone who leads religious ceremonies and is in charge of any decisions. They were very important people in Shang China, often with a lot of power over the king or emperor.

A photograph of the inside of Fu Hao's tomb, with her artefacts buried with her

She was very rich. We know this because lots of bronze and jade items were buried with her.

She was also an army general. On at least one occasion, she led an army of over 13,000 men – in their war **chariots** as well as on foot – against the enemies of the Shang.

Chariots:

These are a special kind of cart, built to go very quickly and usually pulled by horses. They were often used in battles or races.

We know that she was successful, because of all the weapons buried with her. Her husband the emperor, was regarded as inferior to her, because of her success in leading the army and making the Shang Empire stronger. She ruled part of the country. Again, this is very unusual for a woman at the time.

She must have been a very special person – yet we don't even know what she looked like!

Let's think about it!

What kind of person was buried in the tomb? Was she rich or poor? Important or not very important?

What can you tell about her life from the goods buried with her?

What would you like to know about her?

Why do you think the Shang buried goods in their tombs?

Look at the list of things found in Fu Hao's tomb. Are there any clues about the kind of things she might have liked to do?

Ibn Battuta

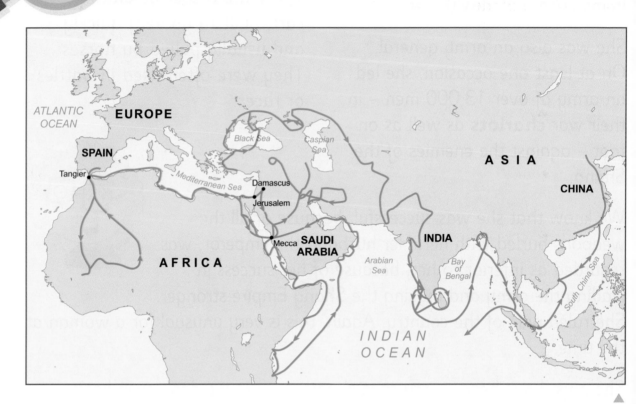

Map showing Ibn Battuta's journeys

Who was Ibn Battuta?

In 1325, at the age of 21, Ibn Battuta set out from his home in Tangier
in what is now Morocco, to go on the hajj. Every Muslim is required,
at least once in their life if they can, to go on the hajj – a visit to the
holy site of Mecca, in Saudi Arabia. He did not come home for nearly
29 years! To begin with, he travelled with a group of merchants for
safety. They went along the north coast of Africa, crossing the Nile, and
visiting Jerusalem before eventually reaching Mecca.

Once he had completed the hajj, Ibn Battuta took a boat south, exploring the East African coast, and then headed for India. He was shipwrecked on the way from India to China and lost everything he owned.

Ibn Battuta travelled through deserts in North Africa; across snow and ice in parts of Asia, and the rich lands of India and China; and across the sea to Africa. He travelled on foot, on donkeys, camels and horses, by barge and by sea-going ships. He faced many dangers, but still carried on exploring. In Damascus (in Syria), he discovered that his father had died 17 years before, and that his mother had died of the plague.

▲ *Ibn Battuta was an explorer and writer*

By the time he got home, Ibn Battuta had visited over 40 modern countries, and travelled around 120,000 kilometres. When he arrived home, the **Sultan** of Morocco gave him a house to live in.

Sultan:
A ruler of some Muslim countries.

◀ *Ibn Battuta met people in many different countries*

What was happening then?

Around about 600 CE a new religion grew up in the area we now call
Saudi Arabia. It was called Islam, and people who belonged to it were
called Muslims. Islam spread across the area and, by 1200 CE, Muslims
ruled in Spain, North Africa, East Africa, Egypt, Persia (the country we
now call Iran) and many other countries.

Battuta visited the Persian city of Tabriz in 1327

The 'House of Wisdom' in Baghdad

Islam encouraged learning and, in Baghdad, there was a 'House of Wisdom' that had a copy of every book ever published. People went there from all over the world to study. In Alexandria, in Egypt, there was a world-famous library. The Islamic world was famous for medicine, science and learning. Much of the knowledge of Western Europe came from these two places.

Islamic countries became very rich, trading with the Vikings, Russia, India, China and Africa. They **imported** silk, cotton, paper, spices, ivory and carpets from around the world. They paid for these with gold coins called dinars. These coins became the currency of nearly every trading country.

Imported:
Brought goods into a country from another country.

19

Ibn Battuta

What happened next?

After he returned home, Ibn Battuta dictated his memories of his travels. How do you think that affects their **reliability** as evidence? His book was first published in his lifetime.

Ibn Battuta was very **observant** and his tales give us a good understanding of the lives and customs of people in the countries he visited. The Turks, he tells us, leave their livestock free to graze without shepherds. This is due to their strict laws against theft. Anyone caught with a stolen horse is forced to bring it back, with nine others, and if he cannot do this, his sons are taken instead. Chinese hens and eggs are much bigger than other hens and eggs. These two stories give us an example of the kind of detail we can find in his account of the countries he visited.

Ibn Battuta was one of the first people to give us a detailed account of life in many countries during the 14th century, for rich people and poor people. He really helps us to understand the world at that time. He died somewhere between 1368 and 1377 – no one is quite sure, and very little is known of his life once he returned home in 1354.

Reliability:

How true something is: can we believe the person was telling the truth, and if not, why not?

Observant:

Being able to look carefully and notice details.

This is a translation of some of Ibn Battuta's writings:

I travelled then to Aden, the port of Yemen. It is surrounded by mountains and can be approached from one side only; it has no crops, trees or water, but has reservoirs in which rainwater is collected... It is an exceedingly hot place. It is the port of the Indians, and to it come large vessels from the Malabar ports. There are Indian merchants living there, as well as Egyptian merchants. The people who live there are all either merchants, porters or fishermen. Some of the merchants are very, very rich...

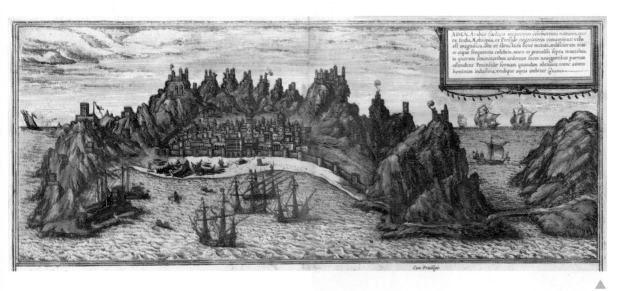

This image is from 1590, but it gives us some idea of what Aden was like when Ibn Battuta visited.

Let's think about it!

Examine one of Battuta's descriptions, like the one above in which he describes the port of Aden. Do you think it has changed very much? Can you write a similar description of your own town?

Who was Henry VIII?

Henry VIII became King of England in 1509. He was not meant to be king. He only became the **heir** to the throne when his older brother Arthur died.

Henry was very handsome, and very clever. He could sing and dance well, spoke lots of languages, was a tennis champion and excellent at fighting on horseback. He loved hunting. He also went to church. He was well liked, but had a really bad temper if anyone said 'no' to him. It was best to keep on the good side of the King!

Heir:

This is the child of a king or queen who will take over when the current king or queen dies.

◀ Henry liked riding in the forests and hunting

The king's job was to keep his country strong and safe from invaders. To do this, Henry made sure there was a strong navy and he had the famous ship *Mary Rose* built. He had to keep everyone in the country safe. Henry needed to have a son who would be king when he died. And that was the problem. Henry had been married to Catherine of Aragon for many years, and they had no boys, only a girl called Mary. Catherine was becoming too old to have any more babies.

Henry's first wife, Catherine of Aragon

What was happening then?

People at the time thought that women could not rule a country – only men. They thought women were weak and not clever enough. They felt that women would not be able to fight in battles. Having a queen instead of a king was seen as a disaster!

Henry divorced Catherine and married Anne Boleyn, who had a baby girl called Elizabeth. He was still not happy, so he got rid of Anne, and in 1536 he married Jane Seymour. She had a baby boy, named Edward, so at last Henry had a son. Poor Jane died two weeks after Edward was born.

Henry with Jane Seymour and his three children:
Mary, Edward and Elizabeth

Henry wanted an heir and 'a spare' (remember: Henry had been the 'spare'), so he married three more times – to Anne of Cleves, Catherine Howard and Catherine Parr. He married six times in all. At least he had one son and heir, who went on to become Edward VI after Henry died!

Catherine of Aragon

Anne Boleyn

Jane Seymour

Anne of Cleves

Catherine Howard

Catherine Parr

▲
Henry married six times

When Jane died, Henry was shown a picture of Anne of Cleves, and thought she was very nice. However, when she arrived in London, Henry found her very ugly, so he divorced her right away. Remember: this was before photographs or film, so until you met someone it was hard to know what they looked like.

What happened next?

Henry's divorce from Catherine of Aragon upset the Pope, who was head of the Church, so Henry set himself up as head of the Church in England. He could now make all the decisions about the Church and not pay any money to the Pope. This was the start of the Church of England and helped to make Henry rich.

He closed all the monasteries – where monks lived, worked and prayed – and took all their land and money for himself and his friends. This led to lots of problems for many people, as monasteries were often hospitals too and the monks would feed and look after the poor people.

The ruins of a monastery

Many people in England didn't like all this and tried to stop Henry. The people argued about what should happen. Henry was very cross with anyone who did not agree with him, and sometimes had them killed.

When Henry died in 1547, there was a son to succeed him – Edward VI.

Portrait of Henry VIII

Let's think about it!

Draw a picture of Henry and label it. On one side, show the things he liked to do, and on the other side the changes he made. Do you think he was a good king or a bad king?

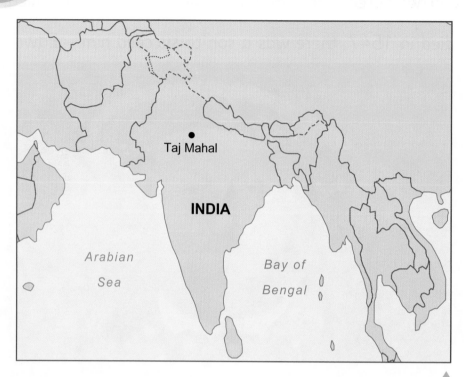

Map showing the location of the Taj Mahal

Who was Shah Jahan?

Shah Jahan (his name means 'King of the World') was the **Mughal** ruler of India in 1628. He was the emperor of a country of 150 million people. When his father died, he killed his four brothers so he could become ruler.

Mughal:
A person who was part of the Mughal Empire, which was in India.

Devastated:
Extremely upset.

Shah Jahan had several wives — each time he conquered a new land, he married a princess from that land to help keep the peace. His favourite, however, was Mumtaz Mahal. Her name means 'Jewel of the Palace'. They had 14 children, and seven of them survived. When Mumtaz died in 1631, while having a baby, Shah Jahan was **devastated.** He had lost the love of his life. He decided to build a special monument where she would be buried. It was called the Taj Mahal. It was built opposite his palace so he could look at it every day.

Shah Jahan also had a huge army. It was said to have more than 1 million soldiers! He fought wars and conquered more land, making Mughal India even richer and more powerful.

Shah Jahan was a powerful ruler of India

Shah Jahan built the Taj Mahal to remember one of his wives

What was happening then?

India at the time was the richest country in the world, owning 25 per cent of all the world's money. Most people were farmers, but they didn't  just grow food. They grew cotton, **jute** and mulberries, as well as sugar, pepper and spices of all kinds. The cotton, jute and mulberries were turned into cloth – some was so fine that no other country in the world could make it. India was also famous for the ships it built. All these things were in great demand around the world – Britain, France, Holland and Portugal all sent people to India to buy all these products.

Jute:
A long, soft, shiny vegetable fibre that can be spun into coarse, strong threads and made into material.

India once made the finest cloth in the world

The Taj Mahal was built from red sandstone, as most buildings were, and then it was covered in white marble. The white marble was decorated with semi-precious stones like jade from China and **lapis lazuli** from Afghanistan, so that it glittered in the sun. It took 20,000 workers – and 1000 elephants – over 20 years to build. The tallest dome was 73 metres tall. The whole complex was surrounded by gardens and water, as well as a wall of red sandstone. It shows just how rich Shah Jahan was!

Lapis lazuli:
A deep-blue semi-precious stone.

The Taj Mahal is beautiful inside too

What happened next?

Shah Jahan fell ill in 1658 and was replaced by his son. He spent the last eight years of his life locked up in a fort in Agra, overlooking the Taj Mahal. When he died, he was buried next to Mumtaz Mahal. Gradually the power of the Mughals declined, until Britain took control of India. By then the Taj Mahal was in a bad state of repair, but the British restored it.

Today, the Taj Mahal is a United Nations World Heritage Site, and is viewed as one of the best pieces of architecture in the world. It featured in a list of the 'new seven wonders of the world'. Between 7 million and 8 million people visit it each year.

Let's think about it!

Can you find out what the other 'new seven wonders of the World' are? Is there a United Nations World Heritage Site in your country?

Who or what do we remember most – Shah Jahan or the Taj Mahal? Why?

The Taj Mahal at sunset

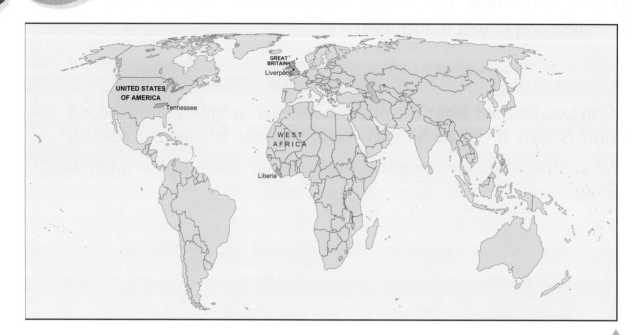

Map showing the locations of Tennessee, Liberia and Liverpool

Who was Martha Ricks?

Martha was born in 1817 in Tennessee, in the south of the United States of America. She and all her family were **slaves**, growing cotton on a **plantation**. It was a hard life without pay – a slave belonged to his or her owner. Slave children could not go to school, as they had to work. Her father was also a **preacher** and he travelled around the area praying with the slaves.

Slaves:	Plantation:	Preacher:
These are people who do not get paid for their work. They are unpaid servants. They are often bought and sold like animals.	This is a kind of large farm. It is usually found in warmer countries where one crop is grown, such as sugar, coffee or cotton.	A person who leads and speaks at religious meetings.

One day, some men bought her father's freedom, so he was no longer a slave. From then on, he was a full-time preacher. At the end of each prayer meeting, there would be a collection for the preacher. Martha's father saved up all this money so he could buy freedom for all his family. In 1829, after 12 years, he had saved up $2400 (the same as $45,000 today) and Martha and her family were freed.

Martha learned to sew as a young girl when she was a slave

PICKING COTTON.

Slaves working on a plantation

Going to live in Liberia

Liberia, also known as the Pepper Coast, was set up as a country where freed slaves could go and live. A special charity was set up to pay for ex-slaves to go to Liberia. It would also give them some land to live on and grow their own crops. In 1830, Martha and her family set sail for Liberia. Martha was excited by the idea of going to school!

Martha learned to sew and make clothes, and also to cook and run a house. She learned to read and write, as well as to work on the farm. Unfortunately, most of Martha's family caught a fever and they died. Only her brother was still alive.

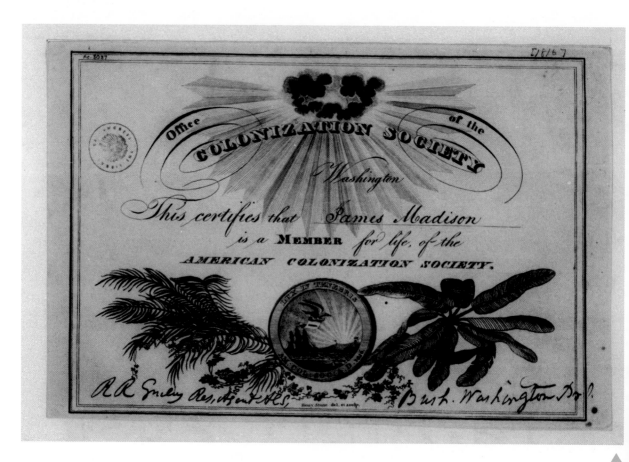

Membership certificate for the American Colonization Society

Martha married and lived on her own farm, working hard. Each week when she went to the market, she saw Royal Navy ships. They were trying to catch slave traders, who were still taking and selling slaves to America. She thought Britain was good for trying to catch the slavers, and admired Queen Victoria for her part in this. Martha decided that one day she would thank her.

Rainforest in Liberia today. How easy would it be to farm here? ▼

What happened next?

Martha saved up her pennies, week by week, hoping one day she would have enough to pay for a ship to take her to England. She also began making a quilt as a present to take with her. The quilt showed a coffee tree, which was the national plant of Liberia. Many of her friends thought she was stupid. They said she would never get to Britain and, if she did, she would

President:
The person in charge of a country when there is no king or queen. In countries where there is a king or queen, a prime minister is usually the one who makes the important decisions.

Martha made the quilt for Queen Victoria

not get to meet Queen Victoria. The **President** of Liberia eventually heard of Martha and her quilt. One day, his wife turned up at Martha's farmhouse and said she was going to Britain and asked her if she would like to come with her? Of course, Martha agreed.

In 1892, Martha sailed to Liverpool. She had her meeting with Queen Victoria. It was reported in the newspapers. The Queen was very interested in Martha's story and how she was freed from slavery, and wanted to know about her life in Liberia. Martha's quilt was beautiful, and greatly admired by everyone. When she returned home to Liberia, Martha was met by a huge crowd waving flags and cheering. Whoever heard of an ex-slave travelling to London and meeting Queen Victoria?

Mrs. RICKS, The Queen's Liberian Visitor.
ELLIOTT & FRY   Copyright.   55, BAKER STREET. W.
AND AT 7, GLOUCESTER TERRACE, S.W.

Martha Ricks as an old lady. What questions would you like to ask her?

Let's think about it!

Was Martha lucky to be freed?

When did all the slaves in the USA get their freedom?

Are there still slaves today?

What would it be like to travel to start a new life? Would you be excited? Scared? Happy? Sad? What would you take with you?

Do you think Martha was important? Was she a significant individual in 1830? In 1892? Today?

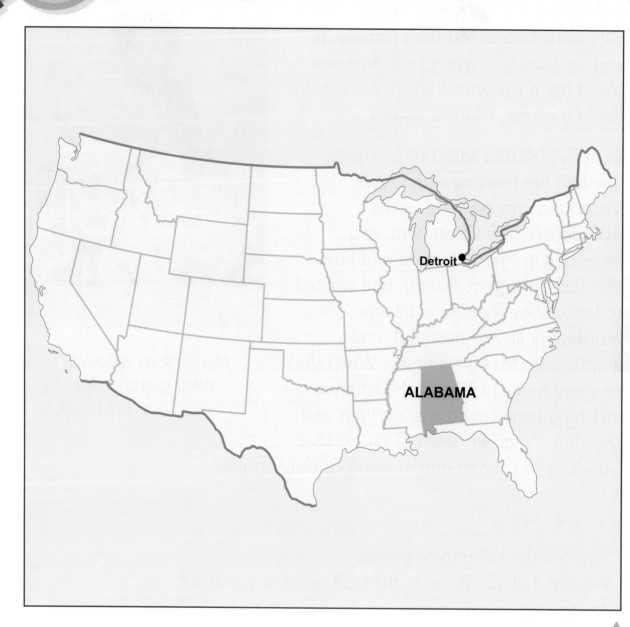

Map of the United States of America, showing the location of Alabama

Who was Rosa Parks?

In 1955, some people in America were very unhappy because people were treated differently because of the colour of their skin. One of these people was Rosa Parks, who lived and worked in the town of Montgomery, in Alabama. Rosa was 42 years old and she was an African-American.

Rosa Parks

What was happening then?

A long time ago, in the 18th and 19th centuries, people took slaves from Africa to parts of the United States of America to work. Slaves are unpaid servants who are bought and sold as if they were animals. They are owned by the person who buys them.

These slaves were black. The people who owned the slaves and the land they worked on, were white. Slaves did all the hard work, like picking cotton, and they lived in very bad conditions. If they did not do as they were told, they were beaten and sometimes killed. It was not against the law to kill a slave.

From 1861 to 1865 a war was fought. It took place between the people in the north, who thought it was wrong to own slaves, and the people in the south, who thought it was fine. This was called the American Civil War. The north won, and slavery was abolished.

However, many white people disagreed, and black people (or African-Americans) were still treated badly because of the colour of their skin. In the 1950s and 1960s, even though it was 100 years after the American Civil War freed slaves, African-Americans were still being treated badly in the south of the USA. They had to go to separate schools, they used separate toilets, and restaurants were split into 'white' and 'coloured' sections. Despite the laws of America stating that everyone had the right to vote, and that everyone was equal, in many places black Americans were stopped from voting and had fewer chances in life.

One day, Rosa Parks was travelling home from work. She was sitting in the middle section of the bus. Black people could sit here, but they were expected to give up their seats if white people didn't have enough space to sit down. As the bus got full, the driver ordered Rosa to get up and move so that a white person could sit down. She refused. The driver called the police and Rosa was arrested. She spent a few hours in jail before she was released.

Rosa Parks travelling on a bus

The news spread around Montgomery very quickly. African-Americans decided to protest. They decided to **boycott** the buses until the bus company changed its **policy** and let people sit anywhere on the buses. For a whole year, most black people in Montgomery walked to work or shared their cars with other people. The bus company lost lots of money. **Protest marches** were held across America, supporting the Montgomery Bus Boycott. All this time Rosa was one of the leaders of the boycott. Finally, the bus company gave in and changed its rules about where people could sit on its buses.

Boycott:
To stop doing something or stop buying something.

Policy:
This is a bit like a law, and guides what people in a company or society do.

Protest marches:
These happen when a group of people who want to show how strongly they feel about something get together and walk through the streets. They often carry banners and chant phrases about what they want changed.

Rosa Parks making a speech

What happened next?

After the bus boycott, Rosa Parks lost her job. She had to move to Detroit because some white people kept threatening her. She continued to work against **racism** and for **civil rights** for the rest of her life. She was praised as one of the people who started the civil rights movement in America. This movement led to many changes in the 1960s, 1970s and 1980s. Four states hold a 'Rosa Parks Day' every year, either on her birthday or on 1 December, the anniversary of the day she was arrested. She died in 2005, at the age of 92.

Racism:

This is when someone is treated differently because of the colour of their skin.

Civil rights:

These are rights that protect ordinary people from decisions made by governments and other important organisations. They ensure everyone has the same rights, such as the ability to vote or go to school.

A sculpture of Rosa Parks on display inside a bus at the National Civil Rights Museum, Memphis, USA

Let's think about it!

Rosa Parks wrote in her autobiography: 'People always say that I didn't give up my seat because I was tired, but that isn't true... No, the only tired I was, was tired of giving in.' What do you think you would do in a similar situation?

Draw a picture of Rosa and label it with some of the things that changed because of what she did.

Agnodice and Elizabeth Garrett Anderson

Both these women wanted to become doctors. Today, it takes at least 10 years to train fully as a doctor – at least four years at a university, followed by several years of special training. It is a difficult and expensive process.

Modern female doctors

Who was Agnodice?

Agnodice was born in Athens, Ancient Greece, about 2300 years ago. That is a very long time ago! In Ancient Greece, only men could become doctors. Agnodice changed that. Agnodice was lucky, because she was able to go to Egypt and train as a doctor. When she returned to Athens, the only way she could be a doctor was by cutting her hair very short and wearing men's clothes. It is said that one day Agnodice was walking through the city and she heard a woman screaming with pain – she was having a baby. Agnodice went into the house, but the woman refused to let her help, until she pushed aside her male clothes to reveal that she was a woman. After the baby was born, word spread quickly to other pregnant women in Athens about how good Agnodice was. She became very successful.

AGNODICE.

Sage-femme Athénienne

(Biographie des sages-femmes célèbres)

◀ *This is what Agnodice might have looked like*

47

Who was Elizabeth Garrett Anderson?

In England in Victorian times, it was very difficult for women to get medical training or to become doctors. In 1865, Elizabeth Garrett Anderson became one of the first women to do so. She could only do this after working as a nurse and paying for a private education, because no university in Britain would let her take a Medicine course. She passed the examination of the **Society of Apothecaries** so she would be allowed to work as a doctor. She got the highest marks of all those taking the exam, but the Society of Apothecaries changed its rules right away to stop other women taking its exams.

Society of Apothecaries:

This group of experts regulated people who could make and sell medicines — like a chemist today.

As she was not allowed to work in a hospital, Elizabeth set up her own surgery in London, including a free service for the poor. This became the New Hospital for Women and Children, and just women worked there. She was the only female member of the British Medical Association for nearly 20 years. She helped set up the London School of Medicine for Women, which was the only hospital in Britain to offer training to women who wanted to become doctors.

Elizabeth studied hard to become a doctor

What happened next?

Agnodice

Agnodice was so good at her job that other doctors became jealous. They accused her of cheating her patients. She was put on trial and was forced to show that she was a woman. Agnodice was then accused of breaking the law, because only men could be doctors. She was sentenced to death, but her patients rescued her and the law was changed. Women were allowed to become doctors in Ancient Greece and that was all thanks to Agnodice!

Agnodice helped many people, especially mothers when they were having their babies

Elizabeth Garrett Anderson

Elizabeth was so successful at being a doctor that she helped change attitudes towards medicine. Gradually, more and more women became doctors. However, by 1911, there were still only 495 female doctors in all of Britain. She was also an active **suffragette**, fighting for women to be able to vote.

Suffragette:

A woman who fought for all women to have the right to vote.

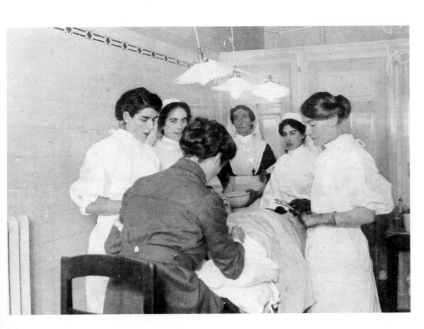

◄ *Elizabeth Garrett Anderson is remembered as one of the very first female British doctors*

Let's think about it!

Both Agnodice and Elizabeth Garrett Anderson had to struggle very hard to do what they wanted to do – to become doctors. How did they manage it? Were they lucky, or do their stories mean that *anyone* could become whatever they wanted, in both Ancient Greece and Victorian England?

In what ways were the lives and achievements of these two very special women similar? In what ways were they different?

Make a simple chart to show these similarities and differences.

People have always wanted to know what is around the next bend, over the next hill, across the sea... This is the story of two men who found out!

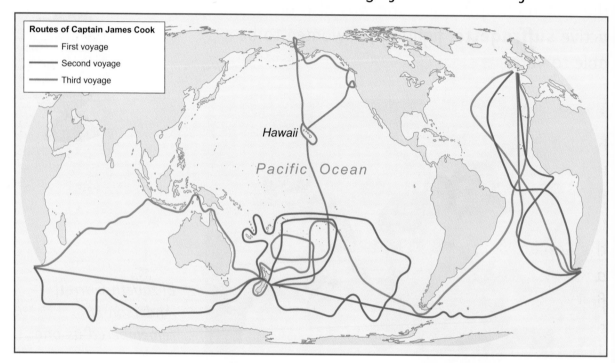

Routes of Captain James Cook
— First voyage
— Second voyage
— Third voyage

Hawaii

Pacific Ocean

Map showing Captain James Cook's three journeys

Who was Captain James Cook?

James Cook was born on a farm near Middlesbrough, in the north of England. At the age of 17, he went to live in Whitby and began a lifelong association with the sea. At first, he sailed coal ships to London, then joined the Royal Navy. He explored the coast of Canada before being sent to the **Pacific** to explore the Southern Continent. Cook became commander of the HMS *Endeavour* and went on three voyages around the Pacific.

Pacific:

This is the name for the largest of the world's oceans. It stretches from the Arctic to around Australia and New Zealand, and from America across to Asia.

Cook took such good care of his sailors that not one of them died of scurvy in all these voyages. This disease is caused by a lack of vitamin C and was common on long journeys because sailors didn't have enough fresh fruit and vegetables to eat. Cook died in 1779 on the island of Hawaii.

Who was Neil Armstrong?

Neil Armstrong grew up wanting to be a pilot. In fact, he could fly before he was old enough to drive! He flew aeroplanes in the Korean War before becoming a test pilot. He is said to have flown more than 200 different types of planes in his lifetime. In 1962, he was chosen as one of the first **civilians** to train as an astronaut. He went into space in 1966, when he was the first person to **dock** two spacecraft together in space. He later became the first person to walk on the moon in 1969.

Captain James Cook

Neil Armstrong

Civilians:

People who are not in the armed forces.

Dock:

When two spacecraft join together.

What happened next?

Captain James Cook explored Australia, New Zealand, much of the Pacific Ocean — even the coast of Alaska and the Bering Strait. The notes the sailors took on this voyage helped to create accurate maps of most of the Pacific Ocean and the lands in it. Many of these lands became part of the British Empire.

Captain Cook travelled all around the world

In 1969, Neil Armstrong was chosen to command the Apollo 9 mission to the moon, and in July 1969 he was the first person ever to land on the moon. As the **lunar module** landed, he told the world that 'The Eagle has landed!' As he stepped on to the moon, he said, 'One small step for man, one huge leap for mankind'. He spent two and a half hours exploring the surface of the moon with Buzz Aldrin, his co-pilot. Armstrong died in 2012.

Lunar module:

This was a special smaller spacecraft which carried Armstrong and Aldrin from their spacecraft to the moon. They could then climb out of it and walk around on the moon.

Both of these brave men went where no man had been before, and where there was no guarantee of coming back. No European person had seen the east coast of Australia before, and no one had ever landed on the moon. Both refused to make a fuss or claim to be special in any way. Captain Cook was more concerned about looking after his sailors and keeping them safe. Neil Armstrong always said that landing on the moon was a team effort in which so many people played their part. They both believed you had to work hard in order to make your dreams come true. When he died, Armstrong was called 'the greatest of American heroes', and Captain Cook was praised for his skill in navigation and mapmaking. Without both these men, our view of the world and the universe would be very different indeed.

◀ *Neil Armstrong was the first man to walk on the moon*

8.3 Captain James Cook and Neil Armstrong

Let's think about it!

Can you think of any other brave people?

When have you been brave?

Look at the four pictures of Armstrong through his life. Can you put them in **chronological order**?

A

Chronological order:

The order in which events happened.

Combined Lower
Primary History timeline

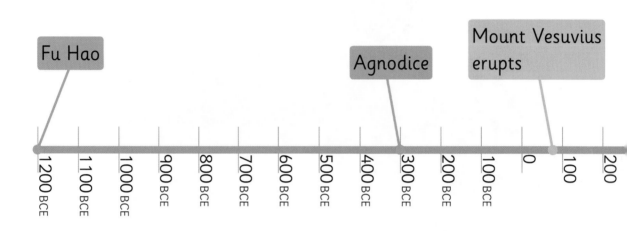

Fu Hao

Agnodice

Mount Vesuvius erupts

| 1200 BCE | 1100 BCE | 1000 BCE | 900 BCE | 800 BCE | 700 BCE | 600 BCE | 500 BCE | 400 BCE | 300 BCE | 200 BCE | 100 BCE | 0 | 100 | 200 |

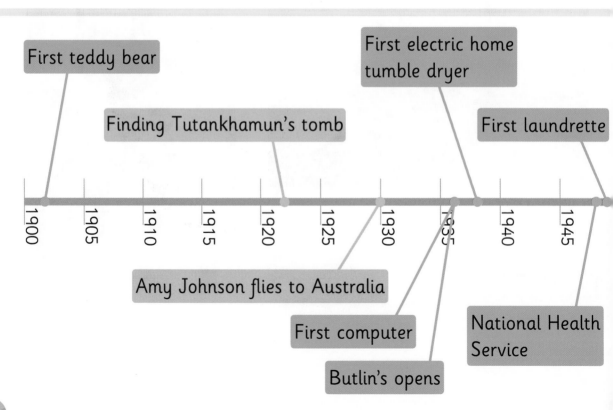

First teddy bear

Finding Tutankhamun's tomb

First electric home tumble dryer

First laundrette

| 1900 | 1905 | 1910 | 1915 | 1920 | 1925 | 1930 | 1935 | 1940 | 1945 |

Amy Johnson flies to Australia

First computer

Butlin's opens

National Health Service

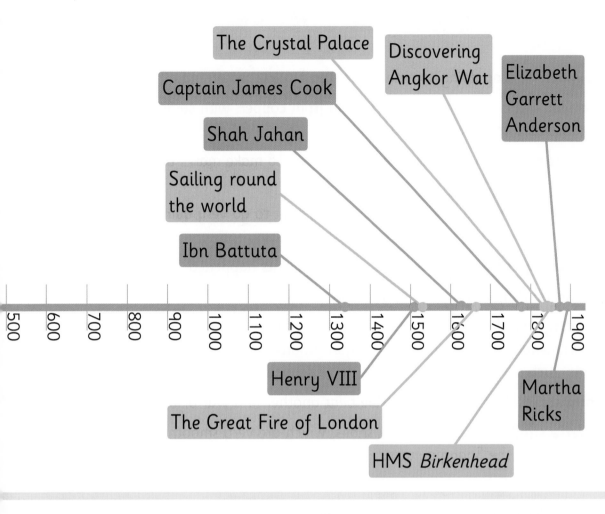

The Crystal Palace

Discovering Angkor Wat

Elizabeth Garrett Anderson

Captain James Cook

Shah Jahan

Sailing round the world

Ibn Battuta

500 600 700 800 900 1000 1100 1200 1300 1400 1500 1600 1700 1800 1900

Henry VIII

Martha Ricks

The Great Fire of London

HMS *Birkenhead*

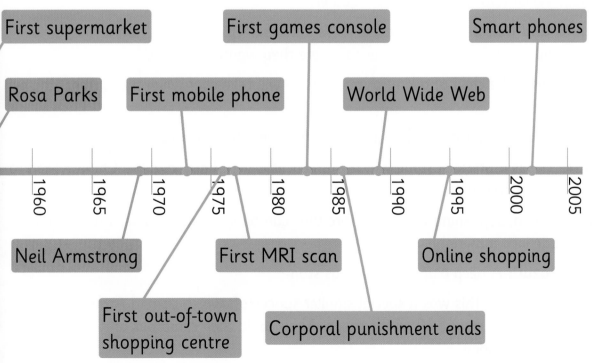

First supermarket

First games console

Smart phones

Rosa Parks

First mobile phone

World Wide Web

1960 1965 1970 1975 1980 1985 1990 1995 2000 2005

Neil Armstrong

First MRI scan

Online shopping

First out-of-town shopping centre

Corporal punishment ends

59

Glossary

Boycott: To stop doing something or stop buying something.

Bronze: This is a material made mainly from copper, with some tin and often other metals added to make it stronger.

Carvings: This is when you use a sharp edge to make marks on an object, sometimes writing or pictures.

Chariots: These are a special kind of cart, built to go very quickly and usually pulled by horses. They were often used in battles or races.

Chronological order: The order in which events happened.

Civilians: People who are not in the armed forces.

Civil rights: These are rights that protect ordinary people from decisions made by governments and other important organisations. They ensure everyone has the same rights, such as the ability to vote or go to school.

Conquered: This is when one tribe beat another in a war or battle.

Cowrie shells: The shells of sea snails, which are very smooth and shiny, and used like money in the Shang dynasty.

Devastated: Extremely upset.

Dock: When two spacecraft join together.

Dykes and dams: These were like walls built to keep the water from a river or lake in one place, or to move the water to where they wanted it to go.

Heir: This is the child of a king or queen who will take over when the current king or queen dies.

Imported: Brought goods into a country from another country.

Jade: This is a precious stone which is green. It is very hard, and the Chinese liked to carve special objects from it.

Jute: A long, soft, shiny vegetable fibre that can be spun into coarse, strong threads and made into material.

Lapis lazuli: A deep-blue semi-precious stone.

Lunar module: This was a special smaller spacecraft which carried Armstrong and Aldrin from their spacecraft to the moon. They could then climb out of it and walk around on the moon.

Mughal: A person who was part of the Mughal Empire, which was in India.

Observant: Being able to look carefully and notice details.

Oxen: These are large male cattle which are trained to pull carts and ploughs.

Pacific: This is the name for the largest of the world's oceans. It stretches from the Arctic to around Australia and New Zealand, and from America across to Asia.

Plantation: This is a kind of large farm. It is usually found in warmer countries where one crop is grown, such as sugar, coffee or cotton.

Policy: This is a bit like a law, and guides what people in a company or society do.

Preacher: A person who leads and speaks at religious meetings.

President: The person in charge of a country when there is no king or queen. In countries where there is a king or queen, a prime minister is usually the one who makes the important decisions.

Priest: This is a religious leader, someone who leads religious ceremonies and is in charge of any decisions. They were very important people in Shang China, often with a lot of power over the king or emperor.

Protest marches: These happen when a group of people who want to show how strongly they feel about something get together and walk through the streets. They often carry banners and chant phrases about what they want changed.

Racism: This is when someone is treated differently because of the colour of their skin.

Reliability: How true something is: can we believe the person was telling the truth, and if not, why not?

Shang: The people who were in charge in China for just over 500 years.

Slaves: These are people who do not get paid for their work. They are unpaid servants. They are often bought and sold like animals.

Society of Apothecaries: This group of experts regulated people who could make and sell medicines – like a chemist today.

Suffragette: A woman who fought for all women to have the right to vote.

Sultan: A ruler of some Muslim countries.

Index

Acknowledgements

The publishers wish to thank the following for permission to reproduce images. Every effort has been made to trace copyright holders and to obtain their permission for the use of copyright materials. The publishers will gladly receive any information enabling them to rectify any error or omission at the first opportunity.

(t = top, c = centre, b = bottom, r = right, l = left)

p4tl and 11b Public domain; p4tc and 17t Lanmas/Alamy Stock Photo; p4tr and 27 World History Archive/Alamy Stock Photo; p4bl and 42 Granger Historical Picture Archive/Alamy Stock Photo; p4br and 47 Public domain; p5tl and 29t Granger Historical Picture Archive/Alamy Stock Photo; p5tr and 39 Historic Images/Alamy Stock Photo; p5bl and 49 Pictorial Press Ltd/Alamy Stock Photo; p5bc and 53t GL Archive/Alamy Stock Photo; p5br and 53b NASA; p11t China Images/Alamy Stock Photo; p12l Lou-Foto/Alamy Stock Photo; p12c Lou-Foto/Alamy Stock Photo; p12r Xiaolei Wu/Alamy Stock Photo; p14 China Images/Alamy Stock Photo; p17b A noble youth with attendants in a landscape, from the Large Clive Album, c.1605 (opaque w/c on paper), Mughal School, (17th century)/Victoria & Albert Museum, London, UK/The Stapleton Collection/Bridgeman Images; p18 Khusrau in front of the Palace of Shirin, from 'Khusrau and Shirin' by Elyas Nezami (1140-1209) 1504 (gouache on paper), Islamic School, (16th century)/Private Collection/Bridgeman Images; p19 Public domain; p21 FLHC 1A/Alamy Stock Photo; p22 Heritage Image Partnership Ltd/Alamy Stock Photo; p23 The Print Collector/Alamy Stock Photo; p24 World History Archive/Alamy Stock Photo; p25tl Chronicle/Alamy Stock Photo; p25tc Digital Image Library/Alamy Stock Photo; p25tr Art Collection 3/Alamy Stock Photo; p25bl Everett Historical/Shutterstock; p25bc The Print Collector/Alamy Stock Photo; p25br The Picture Art Collection/Alamy Stock Photo; p26 dpa picture alliance/Alamy Stock Photo; p29b saiko3p/Shutterstock; p30 Historical image collection by Bildagentur-online/Alamy Stock Photo; p31 Tisha 85/Shutterstock; pp32-33 saiko3p/Shutterstock; p35b Chronicle/Alamy Stock Photo; p36 Library of Congress; p37 Jacques Jangoux/Alamy Stock Photo; p41 Bettmann/Contributor/Getty Images; p43 Steve Schapiro/Contributor/Getty Images; p45 Gino's Premium Images/Alamy Stock Photo; p46 spwidoff/Shutterstock; p51 ©IWM; p54 Lebrecht Music & Arts/Alamy Stock Photo; p55 NASA; p56 Bettmann/Contributor/Getty Images; p57bl Kristoffer Tripplaar/Alamy Stock Photo; p57br Keystone Pictures USA/Alamy Stock Photo; p57t Granger Historical Picture Archive/Alamy Stock Photo.

We are grateful to the following for permission to reproduce copyright material:

An extract on page 21 from *Travels in Asia and Africa 1325-1354* by Ibn Battúta, translated and edited by H. A. R Gibb, Routledge 2013, first published 1929. Reproduced by arrangement with Taylor & Francis Books UK.